*One Dot,
Two Dots,
Get Some
New Dots*

ONE DOT, TWO DOTS GET SOME NEW DOTS

Before you can connect the dots, you have to collect the dots

One Dot, Two Dots, Get Some New Dots
by David Silverstein

Copyright © 2014 Breakthrough Performance Press
All rights reserved. No part of this book may be reproduced or transmitted in any form or by any means, electronic or mechanical, including photocopying, recording, or any information storage and retrieval system, without permission in writing from the Publisher.

Published by Breakthrough Performance Press
1200 17th St., Suite 180
Denver, CO 80202

Editor: Jessica Harper
Designers: Stacy Howard, Luke Van Deman
Illustrator: Kriss Wittmann

ISBN-13: 978-1-938353-02-4

Printed in the United States of America

Contents

1. **Read, Aim, Fire** 1
   Meet Colonel Blaber whose story encapsulates why collecting the dots is so important.

2. **Reading for Leading** 7
   Why reading is the most efficient and effective way to collect dots.

3. **Ask and You Shall Receive Dots** 13
   How asking questions can extend the here-and-now experience for later application.

4. **Sightseers See Dots** 17
   Where you should look in the broader world to find useful dots.

5. **Intellectual Curiosity Skilled the Cat** 23
   The key to connecting dots: Learning for the sake of learning.

6. **Collecting Other Dot Collectors** 27
   Surround yourself with interesting and intellectually curious people.

7. **Collaborating with Other Dot Collectors** 33
   Open innovation programs make this easier than ever.

8. **Collecting Better Dots** 39
   Learn to increase the quality of the dots you collect.

9. **The Dotty Dozen: Tips for Dot Collectors** 45
   Techniques so you can become an expert at collecting dots.

READ, AIM, FIRE

U.S. Army Lieutenant Colonel Pete Blaber, a Delta Force Commander, was stationed in Hungary in 2001. One day in September, he was tailing a mock terrorist around the streets of Budapest for a training exercise when he got a call. A passenger jet had crashed into the World Trade Center. Pete quickly wrapped up the exercise and hurried back to his hotel room where he learned of the terrorist attacks and the ensuing tragedy. As a warrior who had seen combat in Iraq, Somalia, Bosnia, and other places he can't tell us about, Pete's experience told him that there was an awfully good chance he would soon be paying a visit to Afghanistan.[1]

What did Pete do when he learned of the 9/11 attacks? What he didn't do is head out to the firing range to work on his marksmanship. Instead, he began honing his mind for the potential mission before him. Pete quickly began searching for, downloading, and reading articles about Osama bin Laden, whose name he himself had only heard for the first time a couple of years earlier. He began reading up on Al Qaeda, the Taliban, and Afghanistan. He logged into the online databases of LexisNexis to gather content from newspapers, magazines, and legal documents. He ordered books about the Taliban and books written by former Soviet generals about their Afghan exploits in the 1980s. He also read books by Afghanis themselves, many of them former members of the Mujahideen that resisted the Soviets for a decade.

Pete wanted to get all the different perspectives on strategies and tactics tested by different parties across Afghanistan's rugged terrain. In short, Pete's first instinct was to collect information.

Next, Pete needed to get his men accustomed to maneuvering in Afghan terrain. So he researched Afghanistan's geography and winter conditions. His research revealed that, through fortuitous insight and planning, he had already made great headway. As it happened, less than a month earlier he and his men had been training in the snow-filled mountain passes of Montana that resembled the mountains of Afghanistan.

> *Delta Force, along with its better known counterpart, Seal Team Six, is the American military's most elite special force. Unlike other military units, part of Delta Force's training involves designing their own training routines. That summer, Colonel Blaber and his men assessed the world's hot spots to determine how they should supplement their training. They identified Chechnya, Columbia, Nepal and, among others, Afghanistan. But they had no way of knowing that their next call to duty would in fact be Afghanistan, which was not at the top of their list. After analyzing their list, they realized that a common thread was rugged mountain terrain, which led them to train, in the summer of 2001, in the mountains of the Bob Marshall Wilderness of Western Montana.*

In addition to his reading, Pete decided that he needed to find some specific information: how to find Osama bin Laden. In researching Al Qaeda, Pete learned of Ali Mohamed, a captured terrorist who had been tied to bin Laden and jailed for his role in the 1998 bombing of the US embassy in Kenya. He was also highly suspected of planning the 1993 bombing of the World Trade Center and had also served as bin Laden's bodyguard.

During his imprisonment, Ali Mohamed had sought to mend his ways and tried to become cooperative with his keepers. He had handwritten a 30-page document about Al Qaeda's operations and bin Laden's habits. Pete managed to get a copy of the document. He read it, highlighted sections, and plastered it with sticky notes. But for Pete, the document wasn't enough. He knew that anyone who could write 30 detailed pages on Al Qaeda would likely have even more to offer—if asked the right questions. When Pete first asked to interview Ali, intelligence experts told him it would be a waste of time. Ali Mohamed didn't know where bin Laden was, they said. And even if he ever had known, bin Laden would have moved since then—Ali had been imprisoned in the US for the last three years.

But Pete wasn't planning on interviewing Ali to just ask about bin Laden's location. Pete had a different plan. Instead of asking "where," Pete would ask "how."

So Pete visited Ali in prison:

"How can we find Al Qaeda in Afghanistan?" Pete asked. The answer: If he could find bin Laden's bodyguards, he could find bin Laden.

"How do I find his bodyguards?"

"Ask the shopkeepers," Ali answered, "because Arabs consume special spices that Afghans rarely use."

As foreigners in Afghanistan, the Arabs would stand out by their atypical food preferences, Pete deduced.

"Ask the money exchangers, because the Arabs get money delivered to them from home by couriers and must always convert the money to another currency," Ali continued. Another piece of the puzzle was falling in place.

Pete needed to get as much of this on-the-ground knowledge as possible. He spent the next three hours asking Ali questions and challenging him on the answers, to make sure he was getting accurate information. From Ali's information, Pete even pieced together how to infiltrate cities like Kabul: "You dress like women and wear burkhas. In teams of two, no one will bother you because the Taliban forbids men from talking to women in public. Just walk away if someone tries to talk to you." The Taliban's own customs would give Pete and his men cover to enter undetected, faces hidden behind veils, weapons concealed under the voluminous burkhas, with no fear of having to answer men's questions.

> The tactic of infiltrating Taliban villages dressed as woman in burkhas was ultimately used by American special forces in Afghanistan. Eventually the Taliban began using women to search other women.

Why did I share Colonel Blaber's story with you? I chose it because it encapsulates a concept called "collecting the dots"—a skill that every leader and decision maker must master. In today's challenging business world that's driven by complex strategy and innovation, we hear the phrase "connect the dots" all the time. Unfortunately what I don't hear often enough is an awareness of how important it is to collect the dots before trying to connect them. In short, Colonel Blaber knew that he needed to collect and connect the dots before he could call the shots.

The best definition of the collect-the-dots concept comes from a Rand Corporation paper titled, "Collecting the Dots: Problem Formulation and Solution Elements." [2]

"*Collecting the dots,*" the paper states, "is bringing scattered pieces of information into some proximity to each other to enable pattern recognition." This pattern recognition leads to *connecting the dots*, which Rand defines as "weaving together disconnected pieces of information to reveal broader patterns." Collecting the dots and connecting them is how people who are intellectually curious solve problems, and develop innovative ideas and breakthrough strategies.

When we collect dots—lots of them from different places—we can connect pieces of information together to reveal broader patterns and become better problem-solvers.

Despite what we all might think of great warriors who are trained to jump out of planes in the dark of night, trek through swamps, and kill with their bare hands, Pete's reading of history, his research on geography, and his questions of Ali Mohamed offer us a much more realistic appreciation for what these amazing soldiers do. In this case, far more important to Pete than anything else was collecting a duffle bag full of dots that he could put to use in his search to find Osama bin Laden. Pete collected dots—by reading books, reports, and articles about Afghanistan and wars fought on its soil; training on similar terrain; and asking questions of Ali Mohamed—which helped him safely lead his men on life-threatening missions to find bin Laden. And don't confuse what Pete did with intelligence gathering done by organizations like the CIA and the National Security Agency. Intelligence is very important, too, of course, but most of Pete's initial dots came from everyday sources that are just as available to you and I.

Our lives may not be as dangerous as Pete's, but we all have the same vital need for information. For our businesses to thrive and our careers to flourish, we need to collect dots.

The fastest way to fill your head with lots of dots is reading. If you want to be successful and get ahead, you'd better be a voracious reader—whenever and wherever you can.

As Ray Stata, former chairman of Analog Devices famously said, "The rate at which individuals in organizations learn may become the only sustainable competitive advantage, especially in knowledge-intensive industries."[3] That is, the only way to stay ahead of your competitors is to learn faster than they do. Collecting dots—exposing yourself to new ideas—accelerates your learning and creativity.

In the following pages, we'll explore strategies for improving your dot collection approach. Dots come from many places. Dots come from observing what goes on in the factory, kicking the tires in a garage, and visiting labs. Dots also come from other people and our conversations with them. They can even come from watching television or wandering around a museum. But no matter how you slice it, for those with lots and lots of dots to connect, the vast majority of the dots come from reading.

> In the early days of the coalition invasion of Afghanistan that officially began on October 7th 2001 (I say, "officially," because special forces operators like Pete were there before October 7th), many of the things Pete and his men learned through their dot collection efforts would prove vitally valuable. The early days of America's intervention in Afghanistan went exceptionally well. For Pete's detailed perspective on why things in Afghanistan spiraled out of control in the years that followed, I highly recommend his book: The Mission, the Men, and Me.

2

READING FOR LEADING

What are the best ways to collect dots? The most efficient way to collect dots is to read.

Do you read? What do you read? How diverse is your reading list?

Personally, I read a lot. And as a business owner, I've struggled for years with the question of how much I can and should expect other people in my company to read. I'd like them to read more, but I know that we all have our own styles of learning. We all have different interests and different levels of curiosity. So there are times when I have felt rather judgmental when expecting others to do what I do.

But after spending the last ten years studying innovation, strategy, and how our brains collect and process information, I've come to this conclusion: *If you want to be successful in business, if you want to get ahead, you'd better be a voracious reader. There's just no other way to consume enough information and to stay competitive in 2014 and beyond without reading a lot!*

The More Dots, The Merrier

Innovation, strategy, or just plain old good decision making requires that we connect the dots. And while this is going to sound really simple when you hear it, it's not. I say that because so many people I meet don't seem to get it. They don't realize that the number one prerequisite to being able to connect the dots is to first fill your head with lots of dots. Lots and lots of them. Reading is the fastest way to do that.

For example, Ryan Junee, a serial entrepreneur from Australia, got the idea for his company, Omnisio, from reading a magazine article about a dancer. Junee's idea was to build a video platform where people could publish educational content. "I got the idea from reading an article in *Business 2.0* magazine that talked about a salsa dancing teacher who started recording video lessons and posting them online, and charging a few dollars to view them," Junee said. "I figured there were a lot of people out there with a lot of interesting things to teach, but who didn't know anything about creating websites and publishing videos online, so Omnisio was born." Junee tweaked the idea into a more generalized video editing platform and sold the company to YouTube in 2008.[4]

When you read lots and start connecting dots, you come up with innovative ideas, sometimes from unlikely places. Serial entrepreneur Ryan Junee got the idea for his start-up Omnisio, a video platform where people could publish educational content, after reading about a salsa dancing teacher who was recording lessons and posting them online.

From Reading to Rockets

Another example of the power of reading to collect dots is that of Dr. Peter Diamandis, the founder of Constellation Communications Inc.

Diamandis helped launch the multi-billion-dollar private space industry after reading *The Spirit of St. Louis*, which chronicles Charles Lindbergh's epic tale of becoming the first person to fly across the Atlantic. How did Diamandis go from air travel to space travel? He realized it was all about the prize.

Lindbergh was inspired to design his plane and plan his arduous 31-hour solo flight by the desire to win the Orteig prize. The Orteig prize was a competition sponsored by New York hotel owner Raymond Orteig, who saw air travel as an exciting future source for hotel guests. In 1919, Orteig offered a $25,000 reward (equivalent to $335,000 in 2012) to the first person who could fly nonstop from New York to Paris. Although various people tried and some died, no one had won the prize until Lindbergh's historic flight eight years later.

Diamandis had always loved space, and he felt frustrated by the lack of progress in space exploration. He wanted a way to spur innovation in the space travel industry. After reading about Lindbergh and the Orteig prize, Diamandis got the idea to generate interest in the fledgling commercial spaceflight industry by offering a big prize, as Orteig had done for the air travel industry.

History is another rich source for dot collection—and reading is the best way to access these dots. When Dr. Peter Diamandis read about how the Orteig prize launched the air travel industry, he started thinking about another kind of prize that would take people even further into the skies.

In 1996, Diamandis helped devise the Ansari X PRIZE, a $10 million award to the first team from private industry to create a reusable spacecraft capable of carrying three people 100 kilometers above the earth and to launch it twice within two weeks. Appropriately enough, Diamandis announced the prize in St. Louis.

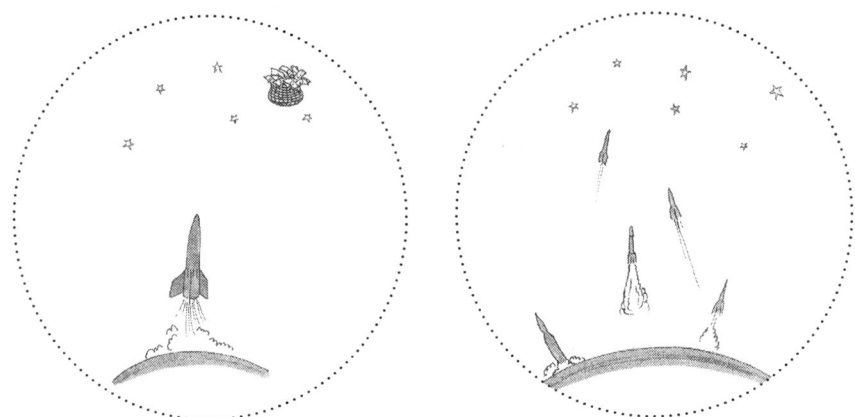

Diamandis, who had always loved space, connected the dots and applied them to the private spaceflight industry. He helped devise the X Prize, an award for the first team from private industry to create a reusable spacecraft.

Prizes like the Orteig prize and X PRIZE embolden entrepreneurs to take big risks. And, the offer of such a substantial prize means that funders and financiers take notice. Investors take it seriously because of the large amount of prize money being awarded and the publicity of winning. Ultimately, 26 teams competed for the Ansari X PRIZE and in the years following the prize, more than $1.5 billion dollars in public and private funding had gone to support the private spaceflight industry. The prize legitimized the industry as a commercially viable one. [5]

Reading widely can help you launch your career, your company, or even an industry.

Four Reasons that Reading Rocks

I've found that reading offers four big advantages as a way to collect dots.

First, reading is an active process—it demands more attention than does audio, video, or other passive media. We've all zoned-out in front of a video or while listening to music, but reading requires that we engage to absorb each word or phrase before moving to the next word or phrase. And if our attention does slip, we can easily re-engage by rereading what we just missed. Reading isn't only enlightening, it's energizing. Learning something new nourishes the mind, like food nourishes the body. It keeps you stimulated, enthusiastic, and involved.

Second, reading is a superior dot collection medium for technical reasons. Unlike audio and video, I like that reading is self-paced. Audio and video run at the pace set by the medium's creative process, not the dot collector. I find that the pace of audio or video might be too slow at times and too fast at others. That's okay for entertainment, in which the director's control of pacing helps create mood and energy in a creative work. But for dot collection, a dot collector needs to be in control for maximum efficiency and efficacy. Fortunately, when reading, you can quickly skim some parts, but then slow down or reread crucial passages.

Third, reading supports random access better than other channels do. Reading exposes you to the world's greatest wisdom from any thinker, in any place, and from any time. You tap into other's minds and experiences, getting ideas that you can implement. By using the table of contents, an index, skimming, or electronic search tools, you can jump to the relevant parts of the text. A picture might be worth a thousand words, but how do you find that one key dot-related word you're looking for in a picture? There's no doubt that visual media can certainly augment reading—a photo or a diagram in a book or article provides richness to extend the text—but reading provides the backbone fabric for following threads of thought that lead to good dots.

Finally, reading can happen anywhere, anytime—batteries not included. That 15 to 25 minutes when flight attendants make you turn off all your electronic devices before takeoff or landing is a great time to read a magazine or newspaper. Whether reading company reports, trade magazines, historical novels, or *The Wall Street Journal*, the fastest and most thorough way to collect dots is through reading.

The Law of Reading

There's no law that says you have to read to be successful in the business world, but there should be. The simple unvarnished truth is that gaining information (collecting the dots)—and a lot of it from many different sources—is necessary for any businessperson who wants to innovate, make effective decisions, and implement successful strategies (all examples of connecting the dots).

The type of reading you do needs to be wide-ranging. I can't prescribe a specific list of reading materials because every person has different skills, interests, needs, and perspectives. But it's important to read both inside and outside your line of work. Perhaps you're a manufacturing manager interested in water polo and want to learn more. Read up on it. Maybe the team tactics of water polo can help you organize your workforce. Or you're an account executive at an advertising agency and collect butterflies and the subject fascinates you. Read up on it. Maybe the patterns on the wings can inspire your next ad campaign. Whatever your choice, read as much as you can, as often as you can.

3

ASK AND YOU SHALL RECEIVE DOTS

As much as I advocate reading, I know there are other ways to collect the dots. Some dots aren't written down. Some dots sit in the heads of the people around us. Sometimes the best way to get a dot is to ask.

Many dots are answers to explicit or tacit questions like: What are people buying? What are people selling? What's new? What's unusual? How can I use it in my career or business? Asking questions is a hallmark of intellectual curiosity, which we'll talk more about in Chapter 5. For now, let's take a closer look at how curiosity and the art of asking questions can pay off handsomely.

A More Complete Picture

Curiosity and asking questions pays off by giving you a more complete picture of the situation. "He asked me a thousand questions in about 20 minutes," said Thomas Teague, president of Salem Leasing Corporation. Teague was talking about Ken Langone, founder of the investment bank Invemed. Langone was doing some fact-finding before investing in Salem. He wanted to learn about the business firsthand, not just from a balance sheet. "You see him in our garages," Teague continued, "he crawls into the truck, he's blowing the horn, he starts the truck up. He's wanting to know what kind of engine is in it, how many quarts of oil does it hold."[6]

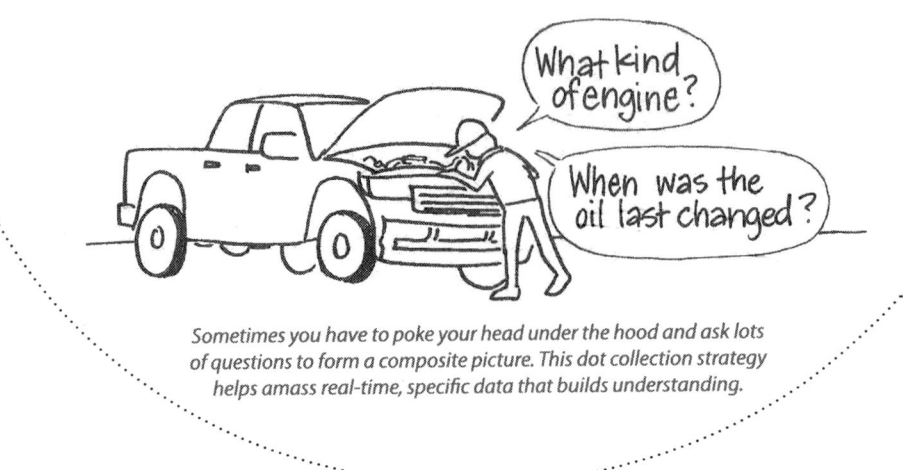

Sometimes you have to poke your head under the hood and ask lots of questions to form a composite picture. This dot collection strategy helps amass real-time, specific data that builds understanding.

Langone's curiosity and information-seeking behavior has been called a "what-makes-it-tick specificity" by business writer Graham Button.[6] It's an amassing of real-time, specific data that helps Langone form a composite picture of a business. In our terms, Langone collects dots to form patterns.

If you're wondering "why bother?" with this question-asking approach, realize it led Langone to invest $100,000 in start-up Home Depot—a $100,000 investment that was worth over $2 billion in mid-2012. A detached, financial-analysis approach wouldn't have yielded a recommendation to invest in Home Depot. Strict financial analysis showed that the margins were too low. An investment wouldn't be prudent. That's the conclusion that Ross Perot reached when he was offered a chance to buy a 70 percent stake in Home Depot for a mere $2 million. Perot, although no slouch of a businessman, didn't roll up his sleeves the way Langone did to ask questions and understand Home Depot more deeply. When Perot's advisor balked at the low margins in Home Depot's business plan, Perot didn't question the negative assessment. Nor did he probe further.

Langone, on the other hand, followed his curiosity. He first heard of Home Depot founder Bernard Marcus when Marcus was chairman at Handy Dan Home Improvement Centers. Because Langone heard Marcus was doing smart things in the do-it-yourself home improvement area, Langone went to meet the man himself. Upon meeting Marcus,

Langone saw a winning trait: "He was—and still is—a warrior. Nothing is ever right. Something has got to be made better."

Langone's initial impression was that Marcus' constant striving for improvement signaled success. But Langone wanted to confirm that impression. So he visited numerous Handy Dan stores to see how they were run. Again, he was asking questions and gathering information to verify his initial impressions and build his understanding.

Langone's curiosity—his what-makes-it-tick specificity—sparked him to collect many dots. Those dots gave him a richness of experience and enabled him to confirm decisions from multiple perspectives. For example, meeting Marcus gave Langone knowledge about how Home Depot would be run. Visiting the Handy Dan stores gave Langone information from another perspective. Asking employees about Marcus confirmed to him that Marcus was actively involved in running the stores. Langone formed a multi-dimensional view of how Marcus operated, so his idea of how Marcus would run Home Depot was solidly based.

Question Lots, Often

Asking questions is an excellent way of collecting a lot of valuable dots. Maybe you're looking for a new idea or you're considering an expansion or an investment. Or maybe you have no agenda at all and are simply seeking to learn. Asking questions applies to all those situations.

To use Langone's technique means to ask questions, lots of questions, to find out how things are run and why. Questions like: Why this layout? Why this product? What's the fuel efficiency? What's the traffic pattern? What's on customers' minds? Does what management says agree with what the front line says? Dozens of questions—and you get the picture. You can ask questions of others, and you can also ask questions of yourself. That is, you can learn from everyday events by asking yourself questions that extend the here-and-now experience for later application.

SIGHTSEERS SEE DOTS

Ted Nierenberg was running his father's business after World War II, but he wanted something more. He wanted, as he put it, something that he "could be proud of and enjoy." But what could that different path be? Ted had a degree in engineering, and he had experience with metal fabrication through the family business, which manufactured the etched metal nameplates found on major appliances like refrigerators and washer and dryers.

Collecting the Dots to Create a Company

Looking for inspiration, Ted travelled to Europe with his wife. While in Germany, they visited an industrial fair in Hanover, where Ted noticed the many booths showcasing stainless steel flatware. The prevalence of the flatware surprised Ted because at that time (1954) in the US, stainless steel tableware was used only in military mess halls and school cafeterias. Why wasn't stainless steel flatware more prevalent in the US? The reason, Ted realized, was that the cheap, utilitarian flatware wasn't very attractive. So Ted asked a question: Could flatware be made attractive and yet remain inexpensive?

Ted decided to investigate. He visited factories in Germany, checking out equipment and costs. His investigations showed that attractive flatware could indeed be made inexpensively on a mass scale. But what kind of designs would be appealing? Ted continued his European vacation, traveling on to Denmark where he visited a museum in Copenhagen. Among the artwork on display at the museum was a set of teak and steel flatware designed by Jens Quistgaard. The sleek, elegant pieces featured were exactly the kind of unique yet attractive design Nierenberg was seeking. Excited by the possibilities he saw, Nierenberg tracked down Quistgaard to persuade him to create such designs for cutlery that could be sold to families for personal, daily use. Quistgaard at first insisted that the pieces he designed could only be crafted by hand, one at a time, not mass-produced.

Ted, however, had the evidence (from his visits to the German manufacturers) that flatware could indeed be stamped with designs and mass-produced. He convinced Quistgaard to join him in a new venture—Dansk Designs—that would produce elegant flatware based on Quistgaard's creations. Quistgaard joined Dansk as its founding designer and stayed with the firm for the next 25 years, as it grew and then was acquired for $75 million and merged with the Lenox tableware company in 1991.

Dansk Designs' beautiful yet affordable products had immediately appealed to postwar Americans looking to bring practical elegance to the dinner table.

Let's see the concept of collecting and connecting the dots in action in the Dansk example. Ted was an engineer looking for a new business idea. He had metal fabrication experience under his belt (Dot 1). He began a search for new business ideas, which included a visit to an industrial fair where he spotted something that surprised him: the prevalence of stainless steel flatware (Dot 2). The anomaly attracted his attention because in the US, stainless steel flatware was only used in institutional settings. Was stamped flatware difficult to produce? Ted visited factories in Germany to investigate the costs and manufacturing techniques needed to produce such designs (Dot 3). With an awareness for American tastes, Ted reasoned the designs couldn't be extravagant and over the top. Postwar Americans wanted items for everyday use, not for ostentation (Dot 4). The visit to a Danish museum provided the final dot—the elegant yet sleek design of Quistgaard's cutlery (Dot 5).

Conferences: Eyes on the Ground

What techniques can you use to collect dots yourself? As you saw with Ted Nierenberg and his process, one effective way to collect new dots is to attend conferences. The conferences can be trade fairs specific to your industry, but they can also be broader industrial shows or events in a completely different industry. Here are three dot-rich areas of conferences and trade fairs:

- Presentations: These can be a crash course in the industry or topic, helping you to pick up the language and the concepts. You might find dots in the trends, new ideas, and audience questions.
- Vendor Booths: What are people in this industry selling and why do they think people should buy it? The answers may give you new dots in the form of new technologies and value propositions that you can translate to your industry or business.
- Mixers: Meeting new people brings new perspectives and valuable networking opportunities. Could the new acquaintance be a new supplier, new customer, or an insight colleague for your business? Why are they at the event and what did they find interesting? The observations of fellow attendees can help you glean the most interesting dots from the conference.

While at conferences, you can take advantage of several dot-rich areas. Don't forget the people around you—observations of fellow attendees can help you glean the most interesting dots from a conference.

Museums: See Beyond the Art

Ted Nierenberg also visited museums, where he found inspiration—and indeed a designer—to help create the beautiful designs he sought. And Ted's not the only one to do this. In an example eerily similar to Ted's, Rubbermaid CEO Wolfgang Schmitt and his head of business development, Richard Gates, attended an exhibit of Egyptian antiquities and came away with eleven product ideas for Rubbermaid.

Make the most of your visits to places like museums, which can offer unexpected inspiration. For example, an exhibit of Egyptian antiquities could lead to ideas about how to better design today's kitchen utensils.

How did they do it? They admired the exhibit, to be sure. Gates said of the ancients, "They used a lot of kitchen utensils, some of which had very nice designs." But Schmitt and Gates went beyond passive admiration. Rather, they asked themselves questions like, "What is attractive about this utensil?" "Can we incorporate this design in one of our products?" These questions turned their museum experience into profitable ideas.

To use this technique, make the most of your visits to museums, art exhibits, and other gatherings by paying close attention to what you see and actively asking yourself if what you are seeing could be applied to your company or job. If you see something interesting, then visit the museum's gift shop and pick up a book on that artist, art movement, historical period, or topic to gain more dots that you can bring back with you.

Be a True Explorer

The broader world is full of useful dots, just waiting for collection. Many venues such as conferences, museums, and well-run companies offer exposure to leading edge ideas and the possibility for lateral connections. Collect dots at conferences and trade fairs, paying particular attention to presentations, vendor booths, and mixers for dots on industry trends, new ideas, customer pain points, companies' value propositions, and other participants' perspectives. Exploration leads to new dots.

INTELLECTUAL CURIOSITY SKILLED THE CAT

In school, in work, and in life, the desire to learn (collecting the dots) is the first determinant of how successful people will be (connecting the dots).

You saw the value of curiosity in people like Ken Langone, Ted Nierenberg, and Pete Blaber. The good news is that you can exercise and develop that curiosity in yourself.

Mark Goldblatt of The State University of New York believes the key to identifying the intellectually curious is to see if students know about something just for the sake of knowing it.[7] That curiosity to collect ran-

Intellectually curious people keep their eyes and minds open—they want to know about something just for the sake of knowing it. That drive to collect dots leads them to gather a broader range of information and allows them to make better connections.

dom dots of information and form conclusions is the hallmark of the intellectually curious or, as Goldblatt calls them "lifetime learners."

Although Goldblatt doesn't believe you can instill intellectual curiosity in the same manner you can teach skills or facts, others disagree. They argue that intellectual curiosity can be grown like a muscle. There's a physiological mechanism that neuroscientists call kindling: an increase in the ease of neural firing. The more you repeat a thought process, the more robust the particular neural pathway used by that thought process becomes. As with any muscle, by exercising your intellectual curiosity, you can increase it.

For example, humans are not born with phobias; phobias arise from an unpleasant experience that creates a neural pathway for connecting fear to the trigger (e.g., the first time a spider runs toward a child). But even after this is established, true phobias require repeated activation of the neural pathway used by the fearful thought. If that thought pattern is repeated frequently, and no countervailing pattern is fired (e.g., that spiders are small, fragile, and easily squashed), then the pathway will fire more easily and frequently in the future due to the kindling effect. Re-

By being intellectually curious and collecting more dots, you can gain a better understanding of the world around you.

peated enough, the person becomes more and more likely to suffer from the excessive fight-or-flight response of a full-blown phobia.

You can assess the state of your own intellectual curiosity by reviewing the range of your interests. If they're diverse, chances are your intellectual curiosity is high. If they're narrower (for example, confined to work-related subjects), you have the opportunity to widen your range, collect more dots, and strengthen your intellectual curiosity.

Serendipity: A Way to Find Intellectual Curiousity

Some people know how to make serendipity happen. Entrepreneur Jack Hidary goes to conferences he knows nothing about—that's how he ended up getting involved in clean tech. He was attending a Socrates symposium at The Aspen Institute when he wandered into an unrelated presentation at an Aspen Energy Forum that was taking place in the same building. At first, Hidary thought the presentation was in a foreign language, but then he began making connections between energy and what he knew from other domains.

Serendipity is more than just luck; it's a skill or attitude that makes a person curious and open to new experiences. Hidary wandered into another seminar and stayed there. That was not just luck, because most people would never have done it. Most people would have carefully stayed in their part of the venue. Most people, even if they did wander into the "wrong" talk, would soon recognize their "mistake" and leave. But Hidary realized that the best way to learn new things and find new opportunities is to intentionally make these types of mistakes that expose him to new ideas and give him more dots.

"Simply by registering for a conference in a given area of interest, we are increasing the probability of a serendipitous encounter that will prove both relevant and valuable to us," writes John Hagel in *The Power of Pull*. "We don't know who we'll meet, but we increase the chances of that value, of discovering things we didn't know we didn't know."[8]

Expand Your Mind

Performing well in school, work, and life depends on intellectual curiosity. Mark Goldblatt reasoned that achievement (in a school setting) is invariably preceded by intellectual curiosity and is an indicator of future success. The desire to learn for the sake of learning (collecting many dots) is a sign of high intellectual curiosity and is the key to connecting the dots.

Scientists recognize that intellectual curiosity is an acquired trait that can be nurtured and increased. You and your employees can expand your knowledge by investigating new subjects and continually thinking about them.

Intellectual curiosity pays huge dividends. As Steve Jobs said, "A lot of people in our industry haven't had very diverse experiences. So they don't have enough dots to connect, and they end up with very linear solutions without a broad perspective on the problem. The broader one's understanding of the human experience, the better design we will have."⁹

You can build your intellectual curiosity like a muscle, expanding your knowledge by investigating new subjects and continually thinking about them.

COLLECTING OTHER DOT COLLECTORS

So far in this book, you've seen how various leaders have collected dots to innovate and come up with new ideas for their organizations and teams. You've seen how reading, asking questions, attending conferences or exhibitions, and being generally curious provide you with opportunities for dot collection.

You may be wondering how to do all this dot collection in your already busy day. The good news is that you don't have to collect all the dots yourself. You can collaborate.

How can you best collaborate?

Divide and Conquer: Sharing Dot Collection Duties

Allow me to share my approach. When it comes to collaboration, I need to be connected to people who will share important information with me and filter out the unimportant. As an example, my chief operating officer and I have an understanding: for

If you tried to collect all the dots yourself, you would have little time for anything else. But you don't have to do it alone. By sharing dot collection duties with the people around you—and agreeing to read different materials—you can cover more dots, in less time.

the most part we agree to read different material. We realize that we can't possibly consume all the information we want individually, so we divide what we read and share what we've learned. In other words, we prioritize and collaborate . . . a much more efficient process.

Within your own company, collaborating for dot collection and connection can be as simple as lunch-and-learn sessions where employees get together for a noon-time seminar. If your employees are widely dispersed and getting together in person is problematic, you can host webinars instead, as a way for people to watch, listen, and learn—and ask questions of the presenter and of each other.

Of course, sharing your dot collection effort with coworkers implies hiring intellectually curious people. In other words, you must make sure you're collecting other dot collectors. Let's look at how to identify intellectual curiosity in job candidates.

When sharing dot collection efforts, you'll want to make sure you surround yourself with intellectually curious people. How will you know when you're hiring the right fit? They're the one asking intellectually curious questions.

Finding Curious Candidates

Hiring the intellectually curious means detecting its presence in that job candidate sitting across from you. Unfortunately, you can't just ask "Are you intellectually curious?" Most savvy job candidates will know to say "yes" whether they are or not. But even if the candidate will say anything to get the job, the good news is that true intellectual curiosity can't be faked because it involves a lifetime of habits and dot collecting activities.

Some companies use third-party assessments, such as Insight Assessments' test of intellectual inquisitiveness. Assessments can include quantitative tests, as well as interviews with clinical psychologists. Some companies rely solely on this method; others use it to validate their own informal assessments developed during the interviewing process. For example, to do an informal assessment, consider creating a list of names from history and current events. Then ask candidates if they know the person. If you do this exercise with your current employees, as well, you'll be able to see how the potential new-hire compares to your current employees on their knowledge of these people. This kind of informal assessment doesn't give you a specific score, but it gives you a relative feel for the intellectual curiosity of potential new employees.

Another method, developed by the Harvard Business School, involves using case studies to test the job candidate. An interviewer needs to be trained in this more involved method, but used properly the technique can reveal the job candidate's logic, originality, mental agility, and intellectual curiosity.

But you really don't need third-party tools or Ivy League training to get a good idea of the candidate's intellectual curiosity. One easy method is to delve into how widespread the candidate's interests are. Is he, for example, in touch with current events? That's fairly easy to evaluate by simply discussing the candidate's take on what's happening in the news of the day. If a candidate is basically unaware of what's going on around him, that's a tip as to his possible lack of intellectual curiosity.

Does she read? What does she read? Does she have any hobbies? Have her tell you what they are. Is she aware of advances in her field? Let her tell you about them. When she's discussing them, does she have a grasp of details? Does her enthusiasm shine through? Don't allow her to just list her reading material. Question her about it. The truly intellectually curious person will reveal herself. It's reasonably easy to detect somebody who has constructed a phony persona for purposes of acing the interview. You'll know you have a great candidate when you get some great new dots from the interview (e.g., some innovative practice in a field related to the company or job) or leads on dot sources (a must-read book, new source of news, or an insightful blog) from them.

An intellectually curious job candidate will ask probing questions about the job and company for which he is interviewing. Was the person who held the job before me successful? If not, why not? How do you measure success for this job? When was the last company-wide meeting and what did you do? What does a typical work day look like? But even more so than these typical questions, which are a start, do they ask questions that demonstrate a sense of true inquisitiveness? For example, do they ask questions about what they saw on your website? Do they inquire about your own background? Have they checked out your product firsthand and do they have questions about it? These kinds of questions show an inquiring mind. Remember that a job is a two-way investment with the company investing money and the employee investing time—both should be naturally curious about the other. If the job candidate doesn't seem to be doing due diligence on your company, what is the likelihood they will do due diligence on the job?

You may not need every worker to be equally intellectually curious, but it seems like a useful skill in anyone who is in a position to offer suggestions for improvements, make decisions, develop new ideas, or help create strategy. You can make a strong argument that in all leadership and managerial roles, and certainly in all jobs demanding either scientific or engineering skills, intellectual curiosity is a key ingredient that often spells the difference between successful and mediocre performance.

Comrades in Curiosity

You can also connect to other outside dot collectors—intellectually curious peers and strangers. Technology makes this so much easier. You can follow people on Twitter whose tweets you respect. You can subscribe to interesting blogs. You can join LinkedIn groups and other discussion forums.

With technology, it's easy to connect to other dot collectors outside your company—and to let those fellow dot collectors lead you to more.

And each found fellow dot collector can lead to more.

Look at who your favorite Twitter users follow. If you find an interesting blog, look at the site's blog roll to see what your favorite blogger is reading. With a bit of search and exploration, you can create a nice portfolio of fellow dot collectors. And if someone stops producing interesting tweets or blogs, simply unfollow or unsubscribe.

Gain Dots in Numbers

You can collaborate with coworkers and friends and experts in their respective fields, as well as competitors and other helpful people. You can share information using such mechanisms as informal agreements (as I have done with my COO), discussion groups, and social networking websites like Twitter and LinkedIn. You can ask friends, colleagues, airplane seatmates, and strangers "What have you read recently? What surprised you?" The point is to use whatever formal and informal means you have at your disposal for collaborating, prioritizing, and sharing information.

Dot collection doesn't have to be a solitary activity. You can surround yourself with intellectually curious dot collectors by hiring intellectually curious employees and by linking to dot collectors online and using them as a filter for interesting new ideas in the broader world. Enlist the help of colleagues to exchange and share dots. By connecting to interesting people who also share your passion for interesting ideas, you can collect even more dots.

COLLABORATING WITH OTHER DOT COLLECTORS

In the previous chapter, we saw how you could evaluate intellectual curiosity in job candidates and connect with dot collectors outside your company. But sometimes you might need to go a step further—you might need to *collaborate* with outsiders who have collected lots of dots independently. The best examples of these are open innovation programs like those that can be found at Procter & Gamble's "Connect + Develop" network and Kraft's "Innovate with Kraft" Program.

Connect & Develop

P&G once thought that it had to invent all of its products itself through its internal engineers and scientists. P&G kept its new product development under lock and key. Many joked that its zeal about secrecy matched that of the CIA. But then P&G realized that its secrecy-

Open innovation programs encourage people to meet and collaborate with dot collectors from around the world. Both P&G and Kraft have seen great success with such programs.

obsessed approach was slowing it down. P&G wasn't developing enough new products to keep up with its demand for growth.

So P&G initiated Connect + Develop, a program that invites outside engineers and scientists into its network to partner with P&G employees to create products. As Larry Huston, P&G's Vice President of Innovation and Knowledge[10] at the time said, "Creativity is really the process of making connections."

How does Connect + Develop work? P&G employs about 8,500 researchers who it calls technology entrepreneurs (TEs). P&G told its TEs to scour the world for potentially useful product ideas. For example, a TE in Japan chanced upon a household sponge product at a convenience store. The TE, after initial research and analysis, determined that the product fit with P&G's criteria for new home-care products and sent samples to P&G headquarters for further testing and consumer research. Results were promising: The substance could be used like an eraser to remove spots such as skid marks on floors or dirty fingerprints on walls. Given the encouraging findings, P&G licensed the technology from its maker, German chemical giant BASF. P&G launched the resulting new product—Mr. Clean Magic Eraser—in only seven months.[11]

What was once considered unimaginable (not only at P&G, but at other companies as well) has become the recognized standard of collaboration. P&G set a goal to reach half of its product development objectives with the aid of outside involvement, much of it by partnering with small- to medium-sized businesses where a lot of innovations originate, as well as with university and government laboratories, and private individuals engaged in research. The company surpassed that goal of 50 percent, and Connect + Develop has become a company hallmark and point of pride.

Innovate with Kraft

Kraft pursues a strategy similar to Connect & Develop with its online "Innovate with Kraft" program in which anyone can submit product ideas. Simply put, Kraft asks people to send dots to Kraft, and they do. Kraft's recent new product, Bagel-fuls (frozen bagels pre-filled with Philadelphia brand cream cheese) is one such example. Kraft had long been looking for a way to make a bagel-and-cream cheese product, to take advantage of its strong-selling Philadelphia cream cheese line. The trouble was how to mesh these two very different products together in a way that could be mass-produced inexpensively, reliably, and tastily. Kraft had been working on the idea internally for years, with little success.

For corporations, inviting individuals and small businesses to share the dots they've collected can lead to new solutions for old problems. Smaller companies win, too, because they get greater exposure and reach of their products.

The solution came from a third-generation bagel-maker, who had come up with a way to manufacture this combination on a small scale. The bagel-maker, naturally, wanted to expand beyond his niche market. Partnering with Kraft gave a win-win for both companies: It solved some of the technical challenges that Kraft had faced in delivering a bagel-and-cream cheese combo, and it expanded the bagel-maker's product beyond his niche.[12,13]

Open Innovation Marketplaces

Now, this kind of dot collecting collaboration can be done by anyone thanks to open innovation marketplaces like InnoCentive, NineSigma and Yet2Come. These services let companies of all sizes reach out to dot collectors everywhere and anywhere.

Let's look in more detail at one of these marketplaces, InnoCentive. Founded in 2001, InnoCentive makes its money by posting challenges (problems) that its clients (Fortune 1000 companies, governments, and foundations) need solved. For example, one of its clients, a foods com-

Chapter Seven • • 35

pany, posted the following: "We are seeking to increase the dispersibility of proteins in water. This will make protein drinks more desirable."[14] InnoCentive shares these challenges with its network of more than 250,000 registered problem-solvers in over 200 countries, 60 percent of whom have a master's degree or higher. Through its strategic partnerships with *Popular Science*, *The Economist*, Nature.com and others, InnoCentive has a reach of over 12 million potential problem-solvers and has launched over 1,400 challenges, receiving 30,000-plus solutions and paying more than $35 million in awards.[14]

Why does a resource like InnoCentive work? Because InnoCentive is a collection of dot collectors. InnoCentive has built a network of solvers over the years. These solvers, in turn, are dot collectors themselves. For example, Zacary Brown won InnoCentive's ASSET India Challenge, which asked for suggestions on how to build a solar-powered wireless router.[15]

"I've been interested in both radios and solar power for many years," Brown said. "I remember sitting in front of my father's antique RCA receiver as a child, listening to shortwave broadcasts from around the world as I wondered how the signals could travel such great distances. Similarly, I remember my parents explaining how the solar panels that Jimmy Carter had installed at the White House could make electricity from sunlight. Both seemed like magic to me at the time." Notice Brown's language—his "wonder" at radio and the "magic" of solar power—that signals his intellectual curiosity and led to the dots he collected.

Brown majored in computer science in college and spent a good deal of time studying the design and construction of computer network protocols—more dots! "I had the privilege of taking a networking course from Simon Lam, Ph.D., who has been involved in network research and development since the 1970s, and who piqued my interest in wireless networking in particular," Brown said.

During college, Brown became an amateur radio operator as a hobby. Over the years, he built and tinkered with many radios, antenna systems, and ancillary components. Brown put all these dots—his studies, skills, and hobbies—to use to solve the InnoCentive challenge. He had studied the design and construction of radio networks, which were similar to the network required by the challenge. He had studied the Linux operating system, which he'd installed in embedded systems and specialized computers such as network routers. Finally, he had integrated solar power into his amateur radio hobby by constructing several solar-powered stations that he ultimately applied to the InnoCentive Challenge. "I had the benefit of already having built similar systems when I wrote the proposal for ASSET India," Brown said. "The most difficult design aspects of the ASSET India challenge were related to the very specific network protocol requirements. Luckily, I was able to find the excellent MIT "Roofnet Project," which had already addressed those same problems and whose researchers had published quite a few papers on the subject."

With new services and tools that make innovation marketplaces available to everyone, this kind of dot collecting collaboration can be done by anyone.

In short, Brown combined his lifetime's worth of dots that he'd collected—during his childhood, his studies, and his hobbies and a directed search for relevant research papers—into his winning solution to the InnoCentive challenge.

Reach Outside to Collaborate

You don't have to collect and connect all the dots yourself. New tools and services help you find people who've already done it. You can post dot-intensive problems online on sites like InnoCentive. Or you can find independent dot collectors and connect them to your internal people to develop products, as Kraft and P&G do.

This strategy depends on openness, which is an extension of intellectual curiosity. It means being open to new ideas from anywhere and quickly turning them into something valuable. Kraft and P&G reached out beyond their corporate R&D to enlist the help of outsiders, such as suppliers and partners and even the general public, to spur innovation.

By collaborating with engineers and scientists across the globe, large organizations like P&G are able to apply their considerable marketing, manufacturing, quality, and purchasing muscle to help other organizations make products that are better, cheaper, and of higher quality. Smaller organizations gain the reach of larger, well-funded organizations through their collaboration. Everybody gains.

COLLECTING BETTER DOTS

Collecting dots in daily life means paying attention and noticing. The good news is that the world keeps making more dots for all of us to collect. The bad news is that there are so many dots these days that people can get overwhelmed.

The Paradox of Plentiful Dots

Our world bombards us with stimuli. Frankly, none of us—either individuals or an entire company—can absorb and process all the tons of information available. As much as it pains me to say it, no one can collect all the dots that could benefit them. There are just too many. The overabundance of information available today makes it increasingly difficult to sort out what's meaningful from a flood of inconsequential or marginally useful information.

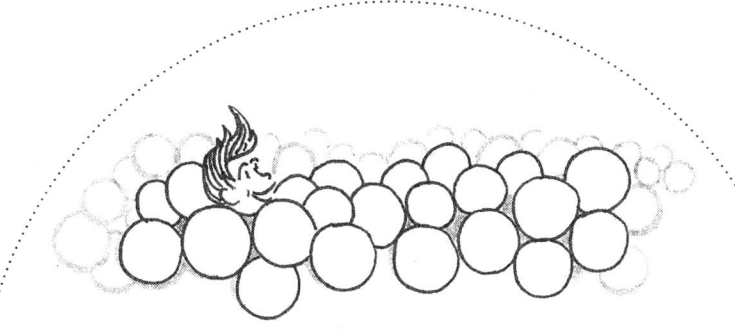

With so many dots in the world, if you try to collect them all, you'll barely be able to keep your head up. Instead, you need to sort out what's meaningful from what isn't.

Two constraints limit our dot collection capacity. First, collecting dots is a rather serial process. For example, we can only read one webpage, article, or book at a time. And despite the boasts of multitaskers, we can't meaningfully read a book and watch a movie at the same time. In fact, studies show that those who think they can multitask the most, actually do the worst.[16]

Second, we can't collect dots all the time, even if we are insatiably curious. We also need to eat, sleep, and exercise (physical health is critical to being an effective dot connector). And, of course, there's our day job. We need to interact with associates at work and execute the decisions we make.

Here we have a paradox of sorts. On the one hand, we need to devote more time to collecting dots so we can create more innovation, find clever solutions to problems, and make good decisions based on a wider array of factors. But, on the other hand, we simply don't have the available time to do it.

Rather than get overwhelmed and shrink away from collecting dots, you can adopt some collection strategies to net the best dots.

It might be tempting to shrink back from dot collecting because it always feels like others must know more than we do. But here's the secret—they don't. Someone may look like they know about a lot of dots that you don't know. But if you're intellectually curious and collect dots from lots of different sources, then you probably know about lots of dots that they don't know, too. So rather than get overwhelmed and withdraw from dot collection, you can adopt some collection strategies to improve the quality of the dots you do collect.

Prioritize Your Dot Collecting Efforts

A couple of solutions to the paradox of plentiful dots present themselves. One is prioritizing what you read, and that's a decision you need to make daily. You may not have time for collecting more dots, but you can collect better dots.

Jimmy Calano, cofounder of CareerTrack, which was on Inc.'s Fastest-Growing Privately Held companies and who grew CareerTrack to $43 million before he sold it, shared his process for collecting dots: "Perhaps I'm too fanatical about it, but at the beginning of every year I create lists of the number of books, audio and video programs, films, magazines, classes, seminars, conferences and self-study courses I want to experience over the next 12 months. First, I divide my list into personal and professional topics. Then I determine what, specifically, I want to learn (or re-learn), and how many resources I believe I can realistically digest. I spend the following year filling in the blanks and keeping myself on track to meet my goal."[17]

Another approach to prioritization is prioritizing your time. In a 2005 article in *The Wall Street Journal*, titled "In Secret Hideaway, Bill Gates Ponders Microsoft's Future," reporter Robert Guth looked at Gates' twice-annual "think week" in which the software mogul would go off on his own to catch up on his reading. He would read journals, papers . . . just about anything he could get his hands to explore the future of technology.

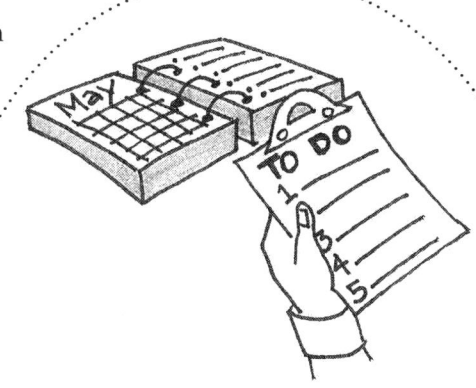

You may not have time for collecting more dots, but you can collect better dots. To do that, you must prioritize what you read, not only on a daily basis, but also based on your yearly goals.

Seek New Dot-Rich Sources

You can also make the most of your dot-collecting time by seeking richer sources. Dot-rich sources might include books on new topics and news digest services. You can even create your own news digest via services like Paperli. Other sources, as we've seen, include venues such as trade fairs and museums that aggregate the newest, most creative, and most iconic examples of an industry or field.

We've also seen how serendipity plays a huge role in dot collection. Some of the best dots clearly come from outside the box. If you only read the same things as your competitors, chances are you won't find many breakthrough dots.

That's why you want to seek out a different intellectual habitat. Wherever you are, it's possible to survey a wide range of intellectual habitats by reading books, journals, conventions, and talking with people absorbed in different kinds of research and practice.[18]

Search for the Missing Dot

Sometimes you know you need a specific kind of dot. If so, then it can be more efficient to look specifically for it. Recall how Colonel Blaber collected dots about tactics for Afghanistan by reading history books on the Soviet invasion of that country. And Zacary Brown searched for technical papers on a specialized networking protocol that was needed as the final piece of his solution for a solar-powered wireless router.

Colonel Blaber's story illustrates a related dot-collection strategy—indirect collection. Sometimes we seek a hidden dot. It's out there but not reachable in the most obvious way, such as asking a direct question or reading about that dot's topic. Instead of finding the dot directly (e.g., "Where is bin Laden?"), we look for things connected to the target (e.g., "How do I spot evidence that bin Laden is nearby?")

Colonel Blaber and others collected dots systematically. Many people do. But sometimes you don't have the end goal in mind. You don't know what you're looking for. Even though Jobs collected some dots systematically, he also collected dots opportunistically and hoped they would come together. Steve Jobs talked about dropping out of Reed College and then about how he would go back and drop into classes there anyway. For him it wasn't about the formality or the degree, but he was still interested in learning. The information he learned in a calligraphy class, information that at the time didn't logically connect to a future job, ended up being valuable during the design of the first Mac computer.[19]

Watch for the Surprising Dot

What should you look for when you collect dots? Here's a big tip: Look for things that surprise you. If you see something that doesn't fit your expectations or doesn't mesh with what you predicted or thought would happen, pay special attention to it. That's what Ted Nierenberg did when he saw attractive stainless steel flatware in Germany being marketed to consumers. Often, the surprise or anomaly points to a new opportunity. If you didn't expect something, others likely won't expect it, either. Rather than shrugging it off, make note of it and collect it.

Let's look at an example that I'm sure you're aware of, but maybe you're not familiar with the details: In 1930, 3M Corporation created a new product for mending books—a clear tape that didn't need moistening. At the time, the word "scotch" also meant a cut, tear, or notch, so 3M called the product "Scotch Tape." The clear tape was intended for fixing torn pages without obscuring the words of the book or warping the pages with wet adhesive.

But consumers found myriad other applications of the self-adhesive clear tape, most of which had nothing to do with mending books. It was used to wrap gift packages, fasten pictures to the wall, repair household items, and make labels. 3M managers did not regard these surprising

When collecting dots, pay special attention to things that surprise you, which can point to a new opportunity. For example, 3M developed Scotch Tape for fixing torn pages, but people started using the product for many other household tasks. These surprising uses gave 3M ideas about potential markets.

uses as a failure of their initial marketing plan, nor did they merely accept them as a happy accident. They noticed them and tried to make sense of them as a set of messages about potential markets. The company began to market types of Scotch Tape specially designed for use in such applications as packaging and decorating. 3M collected the unanticipated signals from the marketplace, interpreted them, then tested their interpretations by adapting the product to uses that consumers had already discovered.[20]

The Keys to Better Dots

Information overload doesn't have to force you to retreat from dot collection. Rather than obsess over all the dots you might be missing, you can concentrate on efficiently gathering broad and deep dots from a variety of sources. By prioritizing your collection efforts, going to dot-rich sources, searching for specific dots, and watching for the surprising dot, you can increase the quality of the dots you gather.

THE DOTTY DOZEN: TIPS FOR DOT COLLECTORS

These recommended tips will help stimulate your intellectual curiosity with information your brain will store and later use, often when you least expect it. The central premise of this book is that the more dots you collect, most efficiently through reading, the more ably your brain will connect the dots and produce imaginative solutions to problems and opportunities. The best dot collectors combine multiple techniques—they read, they ask, they visit, they probe, and they really pay attention. Here are the key tips that can help you exercise your intellectual curiosity and become a more effective dot collector:

1. Read for your specific job
Study your company's industry (e.g., defense, consumer goods, healthcare, etc.). You can stay abreast of what's happening in your industry by reading trade journals, participating in associations, attending trade shows, and through contacts with friendly competitors.

2. Read for general business
You'll want to know what's going on in the business world, which means you'll need to read *The Wall Street Journal* and possibly the business section of *The New York Times*. Both periodicals have print and online editions. Others find it beneficial to read magazines such as *Inc., Fortune, Forbes, Entrepreneur, Businessweek, Harvard Business Review,* or *Fast Company* depending on their interests.

3. Read about the broader world
Don't neglect to keep informed of what's happening in the world and

at home. Both print and online editions of such weeklies as *Time* will supply you with the information you need to know. To get a differing viewpoint, read *The Economist*, a venerable publication from the United Kingdom. The Brits provide a perspective on American business and culture that's unique and often quite different from what you'll find in American media.

4. Read history

Diamandis learned that prizes can launch new industries by reading a historical account. History is useful because even if the technologies change, the drivers can stay the same. Colonel Blaber read multiple histories of the Soviet-Afghan war to understand all sides of the issue and gain insight into the unique contextual factors affecting war fighters in that region. Be sure to read several books and articles on the same topic. Blaber did that to gain multiple perspectives on war in Afghanistan in preparation for his mission. What's more, reading multiple views may make ideas clearer. Perhaps you missed a key detail because it didn't seem relevant, but when it was presented in a different light or with a new twist, its usefulness shone through.

5. Watch future trends

Follow emerging trends on websites such as trendwatching.com and emergingtrends.org. These websites, and others like them, track what's new and what's about to become new in the world of business, technology, current events, fashion, entertainment, finance, and other popular subjects. You can pick the categories you care to follow. Remember to include ones outside your current sphere of influence. If, for example, you are a vice president of finance for a hospital, check out new developments in fashion and entertainment. Trends you discover there might pollinate ideas in your regular line of work.

6. Learn to search

Although much of the time the intellectually curious are like sponges, sometimes they need to be like arrows—looking for that bulls-eye dot that represents the missing piece of a promising solution. Search skills help dot collectors find the dots they need and find second-opinions to validate a potential dot. Learn to think like a hidden piece of information in picking keywords to reach where you need to go. Like Colonel Blaber's search for bin Laden, think about what might be near the target and more accessible than the elusive target.

7. Create automated alerts

In similar fashion, use functions such as Google Alerts and RSS feeds to alert you to subjects you want to follow. Both services cast a wide net and harvest many new dots.

8. Put your hobbies and other interests to work

Perhaps you enjoy rebuilding cars from the fifties. Subscribe to *Car Craft* magazine or read about car restoration at secondchancegarage.com. Maybe you enjoy taking pictures and consider yourself a talented amateur. Then read Professional Photographer at www.ppmag.com. Remember, your brain is always working. When you're thinking over a problem, if you plant enough seeds in your subconscious from the most unlikely sources, one or more of those seeds might take root.

9. Create or join a peer group

One way to stimulate ideas is to start your own small group. An associate told me about a local writers' group he formed to exchange ideas and information. One participant was a business writer, another a technical writer, two were novelists, and the fifth member wrote a weekly column for a large Catholic newsletter. The group met once or twice a month in the evenings and helped one another with suggestions to improve their writing and their market approaches. Every writer walked away with something to show for his or her efforts. You might also find a discussion group on LinkedIn, Yahoo, or the broader Internet which caters to your hobbies, interests, or industry.

10. Meet outsiders

Take every opportunity to meet with others in diverse lines of work and exchange ideas. For those of you who travel, waiting for flights at airports is an ideal place to meet fellow travelers (not just businesspeople) and learn something about their jobs and their interests. I can't personally recall an occasion where such meetings did not spur thoughts that helped me with my work.

11. Visit other companies and other lands

Immerse yourself in the operations of other companies. Go outside your current environment to challenge implicit and explicit on-the-job assumptions. A team of senior executives from a large national bank spent some time immersed in the environment of both competitive banks and an Apple retail store to gather insights about consumer behavior on the front line. They soon found themselves challenging strongly held assumptions regarding how they did business.[21] Company visits don't need to be formal. Every time you walk into a shop, go to the bank, eat at a restaurant, or fly on an airline, you are visiting a company and can see what's working and what's not.

12. Explore open collaboration

Open collaboration is a marvelous opportunity to gain insights into your collaborator's work, as well as your own. And even if you can't use open collaboration, you can still visit sites like InnoCentive, NineSigma and Yet2Come to see what others are doing in this space. The innovations that people ask for reflect the big unsolved needs of today and future technologies of tomorrow. Getting outside your own skin can work marvels when it comes to collecting and connecting the dots.

Sources

1. Pete Blaber, *The Mission, the Men and Me: Lessons from a former Delta Force Commander.* New York: Berkley Caliber, 2008.

2. Martin C. Libicki and Shari Lawrence Pfleeger, "Collecting the Dots: Problem Formulation and Solution Elements." *Rand-Initiated Research*, January, 2004, p. 13

3. Edwin A. Locke and Vinod K. Jain, "Organizational Learning and Continuous Improvement." *The International Journal of Organizational Analysis.* Vol.1, No 3 (January 1995), pp. 45-68.

4. "One on One with Ryan Junee," One Meaning Communicated Differently, August 9, 2012 http://oneisaword.wordpress.com/category/stuff/

5. Ansari X PRIZE, http://space.xprize.org/ansari-x-prize accessed October 3, 2012.

6. Graham Button, "The Man Who Almost Walked Out On Ross Perot," *Forbes*, November 22, 1993, pp. 68-76.

7. Mark Goldblatt, Who Is College Material? *The American Spectator*, Sept 28, 2009, http://spectator.org/archives/2009/09/28/who-is-college-material

8. John Hagel, *The Power of Pull.* New York: Basic Books, 2010, p115.

9. Gary Wolf, "Steve Jobs: The Next Insanely Great Thing," *Wired*, http://www.wired.com/wired/archive/4.02/jobs_pr.html

10. Larry Huston and Nabil Sakkab, "Connect and Develop" *Harvard Business Review*, March 2006.

11. A.G. Lafley and Ram Charan, *The Game Changer*, Crown Business, 2008. p 130-4.

12. Irene Rosenfeld, CEO of Kraft, presentation at the World Business Forum on October 6, 2009.

13. Sara D. Davis, "CEO Forum: Rosenfeld Keeps Kraft From Being Too Cheesy," *USA TODAY.* Dec. 11, 2008, http://usatoday30.usatoday.com/money/companies/management/profile/2008-12-1...

14. Innocentive.com accessed September 2012.

15. Zacary Brown, "I'm a Solver," http://www.innocentive.com/blog/2009/02/04/im-a-solver-zacary-brown/ accessed September 15, 2012

16. Jim Taylor, Ph.D., "Technology: Myth of Multitasking," *Psychology Today,* March 30, 2011, http://www.psychologytoday.com/blog/the-power-prime/201103/technology-myth-...

Sources

(17) Jimmy Calano. *Make Your Move... And Make the Most of Your Life*. New York: Wiley, 2005.

(18) Leona Tyler, *Thinking Creatively*, Jossey-Bass, 1983.

(19) Sharon Roemmel, "*Practically Enlightened Business*," http://practicallyenlightenedbusiness.com/2011/10/collect-the-dots/

(20) Donald Schon, *The Reflective Practitioner*. New York: Basic Books 1983.

(21) Marla M. Capozzi, Renee, Dye, and Amy Howe, "Sparking Creativity in Teams: An Executive's Guide," *McKinsey Quarterly*, April, 2011